WILD ANIMAL PLANET

Amazing Animals

Series consultant: Michael Chinery

LORENZ BOOKS

This edition is published by Lorenz Books

Lorenz Books is an imprint of Anness Publishing Ltd
Hermes House, 88–89 Blackfriars Road, London SE1 8HA
tel. 020 7401 2077; fax 020 7633 9499
www.lorenzbooks.com; info@anness.com

© Anness Publishing Ltd 2003

This edition distributed in the UK by The Manning Partnership Ltd, 6 The Old Dairy, Melcombe Road, Bath BA2 3LR; tel. 01225 478 444; fax 01225 478 440; sales@manning-partnership.co.uk

This edition distributed in the USA and Canada by National Book Network, 4501 Forbes Boulevard, Suite 200, Lanham, MD 20706; tel. 301 459 3366; fax 301 429 5746; www.nbnbooks.com

This edition distributed in Australia by Pan Macmillan Australia, Level 18, St Martins Tower, 31 Market St, Sydney, NSW 2000; tel. 1300 135 113; fax 1300 135 103; customer.service@macmillan.com.au

All rights reserved. No part of this publication may be reproduced, stored in a retrieval system, or transmitted in any way or by any means, electronic, mechanical, photocopying, recording or otherwise, without the prior written permission of the copyright holder.

A CIP catalogue record for this book is available from the British Library.

Publisher: Joanna Lorenz
Managing Editor: Linda Fraser
Project Editor: Sarah Uttridge
Jacket Design: Alix Wood
Authors: Michael Bright, John Farndon, Dr Jen Green, Tom Jackson, Robin Kerrod, Rhonda Klevansky, Barbara Taylor
Illustrators: Julian Baker, Peter Bull, Vanessa Card, Stuart Carter, Linden Artists, Rob Sheffield, Sarah Smith, David Webb.

10 9 8 7 6 5 4 3 2 1

Picture Credits:
ABPL: **Heather Angel**: 53tl; **Bryan and Cherry Alexander**: 38br, 39bl, 49c; **Ancient Art & Architecture Collection**: 30bl; **Ardea London**: 46b; 28bl; **BBC Natural History Unit**: 26t/ Karl Amman: 33cl /David Kjaar: 29bl /Chris Packham: 31c /Anup Shah: 53bl /Lynn M Stone: 49b /Richard Tu Tout: 47tr /Tom Vezo: 31tl, 47; **Bridgeman Art Library**: 45br /M Chinery: 12tl; Bob Campbell: 52tr; **Bruce Coleman Collection**: 10br, 20br, 32tl, 51bl, /Jane Burton: 17tr /Alain Compost: 43t /Peter Davey: 33bl, 54tl /M P Kahl: 37ac /Stephen Kraseman: 39br /F Labhardt: 13tc /Alan Stillwell: 16t /J Taylor: 13tl /J and P Wegner: 50tr /Staffan Widstrand: 48b /Rod Williams: 45c, 47; **Mary Evans**: Whittaker's Star Atlas, Plate 6: 38tr; **FLPA**: 17br, 21tl, 21tr, 23tl, 23cl; /Heather Angel: 27cr /L Lee Rue: 19br /Philip Perry: 44t, 45bl /Terry Whittaker: 43b; Gallo Images: 43cbl & cbr /Daryl Balfour: 37bl /Nigel Dennis: 45t /Clem Haagner: 31bl, 44b /Roger de la Harpe: 43ctl /Martin Harvey: 26bl, 37cr, 54bl; **AKG**: 16bl; **Gettyone Stone Images**: Kathy Bushue: 48cr; **Michael and Patricia Fodgen**: 18bl; **Innerspace Visions**: J Morrissey: 58br /J Rotman: 59bl /M Conlin: 59cr /S Gonor: 59tl /R Kuiter: 58tl /M S Nolan: 60tl; **NASA**: 57br; **NHPA**: 6b, 8c, 9b, 11tr, 20bl, 21bl, 21br, 23tl, /Daryl Balfour: 33br, 35ar & bl /Anthony Bannister: 34br /Martin Harvey: 29br, 53br /D Heuclin: 51br /Gerard Lacz: 47c /Steve Robinson: 26br, 54br /K Schafer: 60bl /Norbert Wu: 32b, 61; Natural Science Photo Library: D Allen Photography: 34al /Lex Hes: 43b /Pete Oxford: 35al; **Oxford Scientific Films**: 6c, 7b, 9t, 9c, 56bl, 56br /S Breeden 51cl /Clive Bromhall: 55br, 55tl /D Curl: 50bl /Martyn Colbeck: 36bl /Daniel J. Cox: 40tr /M Deeble & V Stone: 27cl /M Fogden: 25 /Dan Guravich: 38bl /Mike Hill: 29tr /Djuro Huber: 41bl /R Kuiter: 58cl /S Leszczynski: 25cr /Ted Levin: 29tr /Stephen Mills: 41tl /Norbert Rosing: 41tr /F Schneidermeyer: 25cl /Stouffer Productions: 40bl /David Thompson: 31tr /Steve Turner: 46t /Tom Ulrich: 49tr /Colin Willcock: 49tl /Konrad Wothe: 53tr; **Papilio Photographic**: 11bl, 30c, 42t, 43ctr; **Photo Researchers Incorporated**: 55tr; **Planet Earth Pictures**: 56t /M & C Denis-Huot: 24cl /G Douwma: 60br /Nikita Ovsyanikov: 41br / D A Ponton: 27b /J A Provenza: 26tr /Roger Rogoff: 36al /Anup Shah: 33tr; **Premaphotos Wildlife**: Kim Taylor: 14tl, bl&r, 15rt; SPL: 10tr; Dr Rod Preston-Mafham/Premaphotos Wildlife: 17bl, 18t; Kim Taylor: 7t; **Spacecharts**: 57b; **Frank Spooner Pictures**: Oliver Blaise: 36; **Warren Photographic**: 7c, 8t, 8b, 11tl /K. Taylor: 12bl, 13br, 19tl&tr.

Contents

Amazing Animals .4

Insect Defences 6
Focus on Fireflies .8
Six Lively Legs 10
Chemical Warfare 12
Fabulous Hawk Moths 14
Spinning Spiders 16
Venom Injection 18
Stranglers and Poisoners 20
Slithering Scales 22
Mighty Bites 24
Cold-blooded Killers 26
Flying South 28
Night Birds 30
Africa's Striped Migrators 32
Trunk Tales 34
Jumbo Water Babies 36
Great Navigators 38
The Big Sleep 40
Camouflaged Cats 42
The Dry Life 44
Fur Coats 46
Snow Dogs 48
Monkey Magic .50
Hands and Feet 52
Chimps that Use Tools 54
Underwater Voices 56
Deep-sea Sharks 58
Attack of the Tiger Sharks 60

Glossary 62
Index 64

Amazing Animals

Insects with built-in flash-lights, spiders producing silk as strong as steel wire, and elephants with noses powerful enough to lift tree trunks and yet sensitive enough to pick up small coins - these are just a few of nature's truly amazing animals. You can add snakes that swallow animals bigger than themselves, bears with compasses in their heads, and birds that find their way from Europe to Africa and back every year.

Thick fur over the body, including the face, insulates bears and allows them to live in some of the world's coldest places.

Evolution and Adaptation

Like all animal characteristics, these amazing features have developed by evolution. This is a gradual change in physical appearance, body chemistry or behaviour from generation to generation. Babies inherit many of their parents' features, so any change that makes an animal more successful at feeding or evading its enemies is likely to be passed on. A change that makes an animal less successful is unlikely to be passed on, because the animal will either die or will not have so many babies. Only the fittest animals survive. The changes between one generation and the next may be very small, but they can add up to big changes over time, so the animals get more specialized at what they do.

As a result of millions of years of evolution, plants and animals have adapted to live almost everywhere on earth. We are surrounded by a variety of animals and plants, and each kind is perfectly suited to the challenges in its life. Everything about an owl, for example, is geared to its role as a nocturnal predator (night active hunter). Its big eyes take in the greatest possible amount of light, its keen ears can pick up the slightest sound and its soft feathers let the bird fly silently without alerting prey.

The crocodile's body and habits are so successful that it hasn't changed in millions of years.

Acting by Instinct

Weird shapes and intricate colour patterns help to hide or protect many animals from their enemies, but it is their behaviour that makes so many animals really amazing — especially when you realize that most of them do things automatically. Fireflies, for example, do not have to learn how to flash their lights in the correct sequence, and spiders never have web-building lessons, yet they perform this perfectly every time. In-built behaviour patterns of this kind are called instincts and they are inherited in just the same way as the animals' shapes and colours.

Cats are born with a hunting instinct. They keep watch and crouch near to the ground, waiting to pounce on their prey.

Instinctive activities are usually triggered by some kind of signal or stimulus from the surroundings or from another animal. For example, a rattlesnake rattles when it detects the vibrations caused by a large animal, and the caterpillar of a swallowtail butterfly releases a very strong smell when it is touched by a predator or a parasite (an animal living on or in another). The migration of the majority of birds is triggered by the increase or decrease in the number of daylight hours. Many mammals prepare for hibernation (an inactive state during the winter) when the days grow shorter in the autumn, while the mass migration of mammals, including the huge grazing herds of the African plains, is usually set off when suitable food becomes scarce. Simple hunger, however, can also stimulate animals to hunt for food.

The Ability to Learn

The lives of most animals are ruled entirely by instinct, with a given stimulus always producing the same reaction. However, many birds and mammals, with their complex brains, can change their behaviour by learning. Although cats and other predatory mammals may chase prey instinctively, it is only by watching their parents that they can learn to hunt properly. Monkeys and apes have some of the best learning skills. Chimps can solve simple problems, such as how to stack a pile of blocks to reach something that is high up. Using their creative brains and nimble fingers, they can even invent and use tools.

When a monkey or ape discovers a new skill, others learn by watching and then trying it out themselves.

Stuck in the Past

Evolution continues and many animals are constantly adapting to changing conditions, but some species have hardly changed for millions of years. Crocodiles evolved their protective armour long ago and, with plenty of food around, there has been no pressure to change. Animals have many amazing characteristics that have developed through evolution and allow them to live in the wild.

BEETLES AND BUGS

Insect Defences

The naturalist Charles Darwin's theory of evolution explains how only the fittest animals survive to breed and pass on their characteristics to the next generation. The key to survival is escaping danger. Beetles and bugs have many enemies in the natural world. They also have many ways of avoiding attack. Many species run, fly, hop or swim away, but some species are also armed with weapons. Some bugs and beetles can bite or use sharp spines for protection. Others are armed with poisonous fluids or taste nasty. These insects are often brightly coloured, which tells predators such as birds to stay away.

▲ PRICKLY CUSTOMER
This weevil from the island of Madagascar has an impressive array of sharp spines on its back. Few predators will try such a prickly morsel – if they do, the pain may make them drop their meal!

▲ READY TO SHOOT
Desert skunk beetles defend themselves by shooting a foul-smelling spray from their abdomens. This beetle has taken up a defensive posture by balancing on its head with its abdomen raised in the air. It is ready to fire its spray if an intruder comes close. Most predators will back away.

▼ LITTLE STINKER
Squash bugs are also known as stink bugs because of the smelly liquid they produce to ward off enemies. Like other insects, squash bugs do not actively *decide* to defend themselves. Instead, they instinctively react when their sense organs tell them that danger is near.

INSECT DEFENCES

Blistering Attack
The blister beetle gives off a chemical that causes human and animal skin to blister. Centuries ago, the chemical was thought to cure warts. Doctors applied blister beetles to the skin of patients suffering from the infection. The 'cure' was probably painful and did not work.

▼ **TRICKY BEETLE**
The devil's coach-horse beetle has several ways of defending itself from attack. First, it raises its tail in a pose that mimics a stinging scorpion (below). This defence is a trick, for the beetle cannot sting. If the trick does not work, the beetle gives off an unpleasant smell to send its enemies reeling. If all else fails, it delivers a painful bite with its large jaws.

devil's coach-horse beetle
(Staphylinus olens)

◄ **PLAYING DEAD**
This beetle from East Africa is trying to fool an enemy by playing dead. It drops to the ground and lies on its back with its legs curled in a lifeless position. This defence works well on enemies that eat only live prey. However, it does not work on the many predators that are not fussy whether their victims are alive or dead.

WARNING COLOURS ►
The cardinal beetle's body contains chemicals that have a terrible taste to predators. The beetle's blood-red colour helps to warn its enemies away. This colour coding will only work if the predator has tried to eat another beetle of the same species. If so, it will recognize the species by its colour and leave it alone.

cardinal beetle
(Pyrochroa coccinea)

7

Focus on

FIREFLY BY DAY
Fireflies are flat and slender. Most are dark brown or black, with orange or yellow markings. The light organs are found in their abdomens. Most firefly species have two pairs of wings.

At nightfall in warm countries, the darkness may be lit up by hundreds of tiny, flashing yellow-green lights. The lights are produced by insects called fireflies. There are over 1,000 different types of firefly, but not all species glow in the dark. The light is produced by special organs in the insects' abdomens. Fireflies are nocturnal (night-active) beetles. Some species, known as glow-worms, produce a continuous greenish glow, while others flash their lights on and off. These signals are all designed for one purpose – to attract a mate in the darkness.

PRODUCING LIGHT
A male firefly flashes his light to females nearby. He produces light when chemicals mix in his abdomen, causing a reaction that releases energy in the form of light. In deep oceans many sea creatures, such as fish and squid, produce light in a similar way.

CODED SIGNALS
A female firefly climbs on to a grass stem to signal with her glowing tail. Each species of firefly has its own sequence of flashes, which serves as a private mating code. On warm summer evenings, the wingless females send this code to the flashing males that fly above.

Fireflies

FALSE CODE FOR HUNTING
Most adult fireflies feed on flower nectar or do not eat at all. However, the female of this North American species is a meat-eater – and her prey is other fireflies. When the flightless female sees a male firefly of a different species circling overhead, she flashes his response code to attract him to the ground. When he lands nearby, she pounces and eats him. She also flashes to males of her own species to attract them to her for mating.

LIT UP LIKE A CHRISTMAS TREE
A group of fireflies light up a tree by a bridge as they signal to one another. In parts of Asia, some species of fireflies gather in large groups on trees. When one insect, called the pacemaker, flashes its light, all of the other fireflies on the tree begin to flash their lights at the same time and to the same pattern. When this happens, the whole tree can be seen to glow and pulse with brilliant flashes of light.

YOUNG FIREFLY
Like the adults, firefly larvae also make light although their lamps are not usually very bright. Young fireflies hatch from eggs laid in moist places by the females. Unlike most of their parents, all firefly larvae are meat-eaters. They kill slugs and snails by injecting them with powerful digestive juices. These dissolve the flesh and the firefly larvae suck up the resulting solution through their hollow jaws. The young fireflies never have wings.

INSECTS

Six Lively Legs

Not all insects can fly, but they can all move around and even climb trees using their six legs. Social insects, such as wasps and bees, use their legs to groom (clean) their bodies as well.

All insects belong to a larger group of animals called arthropods, which means 'jointed legs'. True to this name, adult insects have legs with many joints in them. An insect's legs have four main sections — the coxa, femur, tibia and tarsus. The coxa is the top part of the leg, joined to the thorax. The femur corresponds to the thigh, and the tibia is the lower leg. The tarsus, or foot, is made up of several smaller sections. Insects' legs do not have bones. Instead, they are supported by hard outer cases, like hollow tubes.

Did you know? Adult insects have six legs, but young bees, wasps and ants have no legs at all.

▲ GRIPPING STUFF
This magnified photograph of a bee's foot shows clearly the tiny claws on the end of its foot. Claws help insects to grip smooth surfaces such as shiny leaves, stems and branches, and stop them from slipping. Ants can walk along the underside of leaves with the help of their claws.

STILT WALKER ▶
Like other ants, this Australian bulldog ant has legs made up of several long, thin sections. In the hot, dry areas of Australia, the ant's stilt-like legs raise her high above the hot, dusty ground, helping to keep her cool. As well as walking, climbing and running, insects' legs have other uses. Some ants and termites use their legs to dig underground burrows. Bees carry food home on their hind legs.

SIX LIVELY LEGS

▲ **MULTI-PURPOSE LEGS**
Bees use their legs to grip on to flowers and also to walk, carry nesting materials and clean their furry bodies. Their front legs have special notches to clean their antennae. They use their hind legs to carry pollen back to the nest.

▲ **ON THE MOVE**
Army ants spend their whole lives on the move. Instead of building permanent nests as other ants do, they march through the forest in search of prey, attacking any creature they find and scavenging from dead carcasses.

▼ **EXPERT CLIMBERS**
Termites swarm along a tree branch in Malaysia, South-east Asia. Many termites nest underground, but some build their nests high in trees. They climb vertical tree trunks by digging their claws into the bark.

▲ **THREE-LEGGED RACE**
A running ant keeps three of her legs (shown in black) on the ground at the same time, but does not move all the legs on one side together. The front and hind legs touch the ground at the same time as the middle leg on the opposite side, helping to keep the ant steady.

11

BUTTERFLIES AND MOTHS

African euchromia moth
(Euchromia lethe)

Chemical Warfare

Most butterflies and moths escape their enemies by avoiding being spotted. However, some use other tricks. They cannot sting or bite like bees or wasps, but many caterpillars have different ways of using toxic chemicals to poison their attackers, or at least make themselves unpleasant to taste or smell. For example, the caterpillar of the brown-tail moth has barbed hairs tipped with a poison that can cause a severe skin rash even in humans. A cinnabar moth cannot poison a predator, but it tastes foul if eaten. Usually, caterpillars that are unpalatable to predators are brightly coloured to let potential attackers know that they should be avoided.

▲ BRIGHT AND DEADLY

The brilliant colours of the African euchromia moth warn any would-be predators that it is poisonous. It also has an awful smell. Some moths manufacture their own poisons, but others are toxic because their caterpillars eat poisonous plants. The poisons do not hurt the insects, but make them harmful to their enemies.

▲ HAIRY MOUTHFUL

The caterpillar of the sycamore moth is bright yellow. It is not poisonous like some of the other brightly coloured caterpillars, but its masses of long, hairy tufts make it distinctly unpleasant to eat.

▼ THREATENING DISPLAY

The caterpillar of the puss moth may look clown-like and harmless, but by caterpillar standards it is quite fearsome. When threatened, its slender whip-like tails are thrust forwards and it may squirt a jet of harmful formic acid from a gland near its mouth. It also uses red markings and false eye spots on its head to create an aggressive display.

Whip-like tail to threaten predators.

puss moth caterpillar
(Cerura vinula)

CHEMICAL WARFARE

◀ POISONOUS MILK
A Monarch butterfly caterpillar feeds on various kinds of milkweed, which contain a powerful poison. This chemical is harmful to many small creatures. The poison stays in the Monarch's body throughout its life. This may be why Monarchs show less fear of predators than other butterflies.

▶ RED ALERT
The striking red, white and black colours of the spurge hawk moth caterpillar tell that it is poisonous. Unpalatable insects often display conspicuous colours such as reds, yellows, black and white. These insects do not need to protect themselves by blending into their background. This caterpillar acquires its poison from a plant that is called spurge, which it feeds on.

spurge hawk moth caterpillar
(Hyles euphorbiae)

Did you know? Many harmless butterflies mimic poisonous species so well that enemies dare not touch them.

▼ SMELLY CATERPILLAR
The swallowtail caterpillar produces an odour that is strong enough to ward off parasites. It comes from a scent-gland called the osmeterium situated just behind its head. This gland suddenly erupts and oozes acid when the caterpillar is threatened.

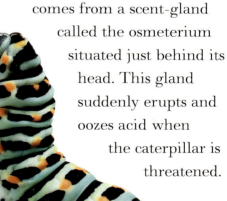

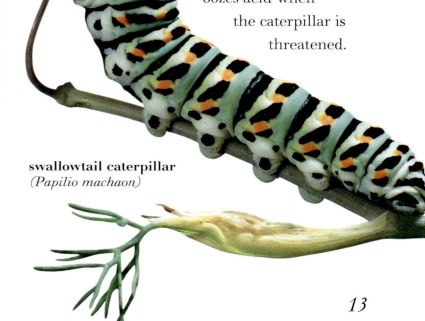

▲ DEFENSIVE FROTH
Rhodogastria moths of Australasia and Africa often have a bright red abdomen to warn enemies that they carry a deadly poison. When the moth is threatened, this poison oozes out from a gland on the back of its neck.

swallowtail caterpillar
(Papilio machaon)

13

Fabulous

1 Hawk moths begin life as eggs laid on the leaves of a food-plant. The round eggs are a distinctive shiny green. They are laid singly or in small batches and hatch a week or two afterwards.

2 The elephant hawk moth's name comes from the ability of its caterpillar to stretch out its front segments like an elephant's trunk. It takes about six weeks to grow fully and, like most hawk moths, it passes the winter in the pupal stage.

Hawk moths are perhaps the most distinctive and easily recognized of all the moth families. Their bodies are unusually large and they are strong fliers. Hawk moths can fly at speeds of up to 50km an hour, and many hover like hummingbirds while feeding from flowers. Many hawk moths have very long tongues that enable them to sip nectar from even the deepest flowers. When these moths come to rest, their wings usually angle back like the wings of a jet plane. Hawk moth caterpillars nearly all have a pointed horn on the end of their bodies.

3 The adult elephant hawk moth is one of the prettiest of all moths. It flies for a few weeks in the summer. Its candy-pink wings are a perfect match for the pink garden fuchsias and wild willow-herbs on which it lays its eggs.

Hawk Moths

GOING HUNGRY
During nights in late spring and summer, poplar hawk moths can often be seen flying towards lighted shop windows in European towns. These moths have a short tongue and do not feed as adults. Unusually for hawk moths, when they are resting by day, their hindwings are pushed in front of the forewings.

poplar hawk moth
(*Laothoe populi*)

HONEY LOVER
The death's head hawk moth is named for the skull-like markings near the back of its head. Its proboscis is too short to sip nectar. Instead, it sometimes enters beehives and sucks honey from the combs.

MASTER OF DISGUISE
The broad-bordered bee hawk moth resembles a bumblebee. It has a fat, brown and yellow body and clear, glassy wings. This disguise helps to protect it from predators as it flies during the day.

Spinning Spiders

All spiders make silk. They pull the silk out of spinnerets on their abdomens, usually with their legs. The silk is a syrupy liquid when it first comes out, but pulling makes it harden. The more silk is pulled, the stronger it becomes. Some spider silk is stronger than steel wire of the same thickness. As well as being very strong, silk is incredibly thin, has more stretch than rubber and is stickier than sticky tape. Spiders make up to six different types of silk in different glands in the abdomen. Each type of silk is used for a different purpose, from making webs to wrapping prey. Female spiders produce a special silk to wrap up eggs.

An *Agroeca* spider hangs its cocoon from a grass stem. It will plaster the cocoon with mud to form a hard protective coating.

▲ **EGG PARCELS**
Female spiders have an extra silk gland for making egg cases called cocoons. These protect the developing eggs.

The Industrious Spider
Spiders have been admired for their tireless spinning for centuries. This picture was painted by the Italian artist Veronese in the 1500s. He wanted to depict the virtues of the great city of Venice, whose wealth was based on trade. To represent hard work and industry he painted this figure of a woman holding up a spider in its web.

▲ **A SILKEN RETREAT**
Many spiders build silk shelters or nests. The tube-web spider occupies a hole in the bark of a tree. Its tube-shaped retreat has a number of trip lines radiating out like the spokes of a wheel. If an insect trips over a line, the spider rushes out to grab and eat it.

▲ STICKY SILK

Silk oozes out through a spider's spinnerets. Two or more kinds of silk can be spun at the same time. Orb-web spiders produce gummy silk to make their webs sticky.

SPINNERETS ▶

A spider's spinnerets have many fine tubes on the end. The smaller tubes, or spools, produce finer silk for wrapping prey. Larger tubes, called spigots, produce coarser strands for webs.

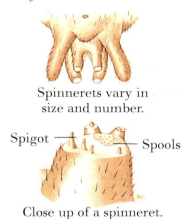

Spinnerets vary in size and number.

Spigot — Spools

Close up of a spinneret.

▲ FOOD PARCEL

A garden spider (*Araneus*) stops a grasshopper from escaping by wrapping it in silk. The prey is also paralysed by the spider's poisonous bite. Most spiders make silk for wrapping prey.

▲ COMBING OUT SILK

This lace-weaver spider is using its back legs to comb out a special silk. It has an extra spinning organ (the cribellum) in front of its spinnerets that produces very fine silk.

▲ VELCRO SILK

The lacy webs made by cribellate spiders contain tiny loops, like velcro, that catch on the hairs and bristles of insect prey. Combined in bands with normal silk, the fluffy-looking cribellate silk stops insect prey from escaping.

SPIDERS

Venom Injection

Nearly all spiders use poison for defence and to kill or paralyse their prey. Spider poison is called venom. It is injected into prey through needle-like jaws called fangs. There are two main kinds of venom that can have serious effects. Most dangerous spiders, such as widow spiders, produce nerve poison to paralyse victims quickly. The other kind of venom works more slowly, destroying tissues and causing ulcers and gangrene. It is made by the recluse spiders. Spider venom is intended to kill insects and small prey – only about 30 spider species are dangerous to people.

▲ **VIOLIN SPIDER**
This small brown spider is one of the recluse spiders. It lives in people's homes and may crawl into clothes and bedding. Bites from recluse spiders in America have caused ulcers, especially near the wound, and even death in humans.

▲ **WANDERING KILLER**
The Brazilian wandering spider is a large hunting spider that produces one of the most toxic venoms of all spiders. If disturbed it raises its front legs to expose its threatening jaws. It has the largest venom glands of any spider (up to 10mm long), which hold enough venom to kill 225 mice. Several people have died from this spider's bite.

The Spider Dance
In the Middle Ages people from Taranto in southern Italy called the large wolf spider (Lycosa narbonensis) *the tarantula. They believed the venom of this spider's bite could only be flushed from the body by doing the tarantella, a lively dance. However, Lycosa's bite is not serious. An epidemic of dangerous spider bites at the time was probably caused by the malmignatte spider.*

▲ SUDDEN DEATH

Crab spiders do not spin webs so they need to kill their prey quickly. They usually inject their venom into the main nerve cords in the neck where the poison will get to work most rapidly. They are able to kill insects much larger than themselves, such as bees.

WIDOW SPIDER ▶

The Australian red-back spider is one of the world's most deadly widow spiders. Widow spiders are named after the female's habit of eating the male after mating. Only female widow spiders are dangerous to people – the much smaller male's fangs are far too tiny to break through human skin.

Did you know? A black widow's venom is 15 times more poisonous than a rattlesnake's.

▲ GENTLE GIANT

Tarantulas look very dangerous and have huge fangs, but at worst their bite is no more painful than a wasp sting. They have small venom glands and are unlikely to bite unless handled roughly. They use venom to digest their prey.

▲ LETHAL BITE

The black widow is a North American spider with venom powerful enough to kill a person (although medicines can now prevent this happening). These shy spiders hide away if disturbed, but like to live near people. One of the main ingredients in their venom knocks out insects and another paralyses mammals and birds by damaging their nervous systems.

Stranglers and Poisoners

Most snakes kill their prey before eating it. Snakes kill by using poison or by squeezing their prey to death. Snakes that squeeze are called constrictors and they stop their prey from breathing. Victims die from suffocation or shock. To swallow living or dead prey, a snake opens its jaws wide. Lots of slimy saliva helps the meal to slide down. After eating, a snake yawns widely to put its jaws back into place. Digestion can take several days, or even weeks.

American racer
(*Coluber constrictor*)

▲ BIG MOUTHFUL
This American racer is trying to swallow a living frog. The frog has puffed up its body with air to make it more difficult for the snake to swallow.

▲ AT FULL STRETCH
This fer-de-lance snake is at full stretch to swallow its huge meal. It is a large pit viper that kills with poison.

▲ SWALLOWING A MEAL
The copperhead, a poisonous snake from North America, holds on to a dead mouse.

▲ **KILLING TIME**
A crocodile is slowly squeezed to death by a rock python. The time it takes for a constricting snake to kill its prey depends on the size of the prey and how strong it is.

Did you know? King cobras sometimes kill Indian elephants by biting them on the trunk.

Spotted python
(Liasis maculosus)

▶ **COILED KILLER**
The spotted python sinks its teeth into its victim. It throws coils around the victim's body, and tightens its grip until the animal cannot breathe.

▲ **HEAD-FIRST**
A whiptail wallaby's legs disappear inside a carpet python's body. Snakes usually try to swallow their prey head-first so that legs, wings or scales fold back. This helps the victim to slide into the snake's stomach more easily.

▼ **BREATHING TUBE**
An African python shows its breathing tube. As the snake eats, the windpipe moves to the front of the mouth so that air can get to and from the lungs.

Slithering Scales

▼ POINTED SNOUT
As its name suggests, the European nose-horned viper has a strange horn on its nose. The horn is made up of small scales that lie over a bony or fleshy lump sticking out at the end of the nose.

Nose-horned viper
(Vipera ammodytes)

A snake's scales are extra-thick pieces of skin. Like a suit of armour, the scales protect the snake from knocks and scrapes as it moves. The scales also allow the skin to stretch when the snake moves or feeds. Scales are usually made of a horny substance, called keratin. Every part of a snake's body is covered in scales, even the eyes. Every so often a snake grows a new skin underneath its old one. Then it wriggles out of the dead skin.

▼ SCUTES
Most snakes have a row of broad scales, called scutes, underneath their bodies. The scutes go across a snake's body from side to side, and end where the tail starts. Scutes help snakes to grip the ground.

Corn snake's scutes

▼ WARNING RATTLE
The rattlesnake has a number of hollow tail-tips that make a buzzing sound when shaken. The snake uses this sound to warn other animals. When it sheds its skin, a section at the end of the tail is left, adding another piece to the rattle.

Rattlesnake's rattle

▶ **SKIN SCALES**

When a snake's skin is stretched, the scales pull apart so that you can see the skin between them. The scales grow out of the top layer of the skin, called the epidermis. There are different kinds of scales. Smooth scales make it easier for the snake to squeeze through tight spaces.

Look closely at the rough scales of the puff adder (left) and you will see a raised ridge, or keel, sticking up in the middle of each one.

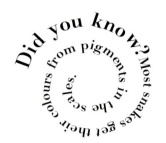

Did you know? Most snakes get their colours from pigments in the scales.

Corn snake's scales

The wart snake (right) uses its scales to grip its food. Its rough scales help the snake to keep a firm hold on slippery fish until it can swallow them. The snake's scales do not overlap.

The green scales and stretched blue skin (left) belong to a boa. These smooth scales help the boa to slide over leafy branches. Burrowing snakes have smooth scales so that they can slip through soil.

Eternal Youth

A poem written in the Middle East about 3,700 years ago tells a story about why snakes can shed their skins. The hero of the poem is Gilgamesh (shown here holding a captured lion). He finds a magic plant that will make a person young again. While he is washing at a pool, a snake eats the plant. Since then, snakes have been able to shed their skins and become young again. But people have never found the plant – which is why they always grow old and die.

Did you know? The hairy bush viper has pointed scales with curled tips, making it look hairy.

Mighty Bites

The huge jaws of a crocodile and its impressive spiky teeth are lethal weapons for catching prey. Crocodiles and their relatives (crocodilians) have two or three times as many teeth as a human. They have sharp, pointed teeth at the front of the mouth that are used to pierce and grip prey. The force of the jaws closing drives these teeth, like a row of knives, deep into a victim's flesh. The short, blunt teeth at the back of the mouth are used for crushing prey. Crocodilian teeth are no good for chewing food, and the jaws cannot be moved sideways to chew either. Food has to be swallowed whole, or torn into chunks. The teeth are constantly growing. If a tooth falls out, a new one grows through to replace it.

▲ MEGA JAWS
The jaws of a Nile crocodile close with tremendous force. They sink into their prey with many tonnes of crushing pressure, but the muscles that open the jaws are weak. A thick elastic band over the snout can easily hold a crocodile's jaws shut.

◀ NEW TEETH FOR OLD
Each tooth is set in a socket and held in place by a connecting layer of tissue. Throughout a crocodile's life, the old teeth fall out and new teeth underneath take their place. Teeth last up to two years before falling out. Alternate teeth are replaced together, so that not all the teeth in one part of the mouth are lost at once.

◀ **LOTS OF TEETH**

The gharial has more teeth than any other crocodilian, around 110. Its teeth are also smaller than those of other crocodilians and are all the same size. The narrow, beak-like snout and long, thin teeth of the gharial are geared to grabbing fish with a sweeping sideways movement of the head. The sharp teeth interlock to trap and impale the slippery prey.

CHARMING

Crocodilian teeth are sometimes made into necklaces. People wear them as decoration or lucky charms. In South America, the Montana people of Peru believe they will be protected from poisoning by wearing a crocodile tooth.

▲ **BABY TEETH**

A baby American alligator is born with a full set of 80 teeth when it hatches from its egg. Baby teeth are not as sharp as adult teeth and are more fragile. They are like tiny needles. In young crocodiles, the teeth at the back of the mouth usually fall out first. In adults it is the teeth at the front that fall out more often.

▶ **GRABBING TEETH**

A Nile crocodile grasps a lump of prey ready for swallowing. If prey is too large to swallow whole, the crocodile grips the food firmly in its teeth and shakes its head hard so that any unwanted pieces are shaken off.

A Nile crocodile has 68 teeth lining its huge jaws.

Cold-blooded Killers

Soon after the sun rises, the first alligators heave themselves out of the river and flop down on the bank. The banks fill up quickly as more alligators join the first, warming their scaly bodies in the sun's rays. As the hours go by and the day gets hotter, the alligators open their toothy jaws wide to cool down. Later in the day, they may go for a swim or crawl into the shade to cool off. As the air chills at night, the alligators slip back into the water again. This is because water stays warmer for longer at night than the land.

Crocodiles and their relatives (crocodilians) are cold-blooded, which means that their body temperature varies with outside temperatures. To warm up or cool down, they move to warm or cool places. Their ideal body temperature is between 30 and 35°C.

▲ MUD PACK
A spectacled caiman is buried deep in the mud to keep cool during the hot, dry season. Mud is like water and does not get as hot or as cold as dry land. It also helps to keep the caiman's scaly skin free from bloodsucking parasites.

◀ SOLAR PANELS
The crested scutes on the tail of a crocodilian are like the bony plates on armoured dinosaurs. They act like solar panels, picking up heat when the animal basks in the sun. The scutes can also move apart fractionally to let as much heat as possible escape from the body to cool it down.

◀ UNDER THE ICE

An alligator can survive under ice if it keeps a breathing hole open. Of all crocodilians, only alligators stay active at temperatures as low as 12 or 15°C. They do not eat, however, because the temperature is too low for their digestions to work.

▼ OPEN WIDE

While a Nile crocodile suns itself on a rock it also opens its mouth in a wide gape. Gaping helps to prevent the crocodile becoming too hot. The breeze flowing over the wide, wet surfaces of the mouth and tongue dries its moisture and, in turn, cools off its blood. If you lick your finger and blow on it softly, you will notice that it feels a lot cooler.

▲ ALLIGATOR DAYS

Alligators follow a distinct daily routine when the weather is good, moving in and out of the water at regular intervals. If they are disturbed they will also go into the water. In winter, alligators retreat into dens and become sleepy because their blood cools and slows them down.

LESS NEED TO FEED ▶

Being cold-blooded can be quite useful. These alligators can bask in the sun without having to eat very much or very often. Warm-blooded animals such as mammals have to eat regularly. They need to eat about five times as much food as crocodilians to keep their bodies warm.

Flying South

Every bird of prey maintains a territory in which it can feed and breed. There is usually no room for the parents' offspring, so they have to forge a new territory themselves. The parents may stay in their breeding area all year long if there is enough food. If not, they may migrate (move away) to somewhere warmer in winter, because sometimes their prey have themselves migrated. For example, peregrines that bred on the tundra in northern Europe fly some 14,000 kilometres to spend winter in South Africa.

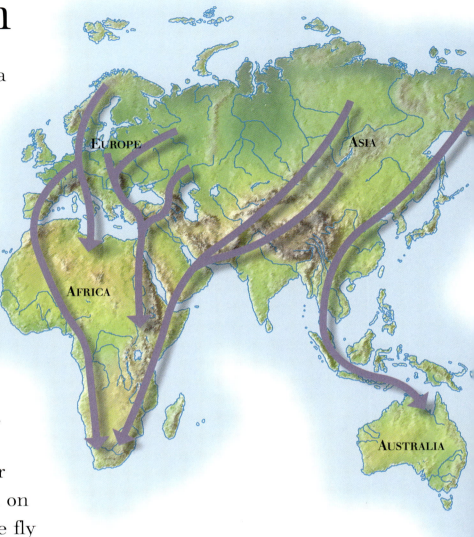

◀ SOON TIME TO LEAVE
The rough-legged buzzard is slightly larger than its close relative, the common buzzard. It breeds in far northern regions of the world in the spring, both on the treeless tundra and the forested taiga. In the autumn, it migrates south to escape the freezing temperatures of the Arctic winter.

▲ FLIGHT PATHS
Birds avoid migrating over large stretches of water. There are fewer uplifting air currents over water than there are over land. So, many migration routes pass through regions where there is a convenient land bridge or a short sea crossing. Panama, in Central America, is one such area. Gibraltar, in southern Europe, is another.

FLYING SOUTH

▼ JUST PASSING THROUGH
This sooty falcon was spotted on its way south to the island of Madagascar, where it spends the winter. In spring, it will return to north-east Africa or Israel to breed.

sooty falcon (*Falco concolor*)

KEY
→ migration routes of birds of prey

▲ KITE FLYING
The red kite is unmistakable, with its rust-brown belly and white wing patches. There are about 100 red kites in Wales. Unlike many of their European cousins, those that breed in Wales do not usually migrate south in winter.

▲ LONG DISTANCE TRAVELLERS
Graceful kites fly over an Indian village during their annual migration from Asia to warmer winter quarters in southern Africa. They will cover hundreds of kilometres a day.

Night Birds

Owls are supreme night hunters with bodies perfectly adapted for hunting in the dark. For one thing, they fly silently. The flight feathers on their wings are covered with a fine down to muffle the sound of air passing over them. Owls' eyes are particularly adapted for night vision. They contain many more rods than the eyes of other bird species. Rods are the structures that make eyes sensitive to light. An owl's hearing is superb too. The rings of fine feathers owls have around their eyes help to channel sounds into the ears. The ears themselves are surrounded by flaps of skin, which can be moved to pinpoint the sources of sounds precisely.

A few other meat-eating birds also hunt after sundown. They include the bat hawk of Africa and Asia, which catches and eats bats and insects while on the wing.

▲ **GETTING A GRIP**
Like all owls, the barn owl has powerful claws for attacking and gripping prey. The outer toe can be moved backwards and forwards to change grip.

▲ **GHOSTLY FACE**
Of all the owls, the barn owl has the most prominent round face – this is called a facial disc. This gives it a rather ghostly appearance. The disc is formed of short, stiff feathers.

Wise Owls
For centuries, owls have had a reputation for being wise birds. This came about because in Greek mythology, the little owl was the sacred bird of the goddess of wisdom, Athena. She gave her name to Greece's capital city, Athens. The best-known coin of the ancient Greek world was issued in Athens and featured an owl.

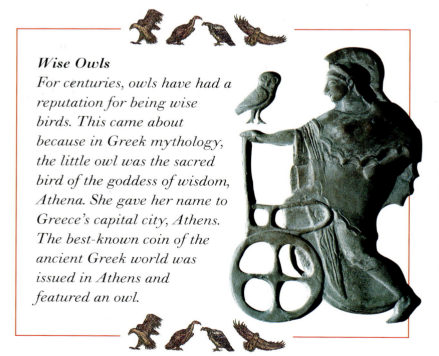

NIGHT BIRDS

▲ THE WORLD'S LARGEST OWL
A European eagle owl stands over a red fox left out for it as bait. It looks around warily before beginning to eat. The eagle owl is a fierce predator, and will hunt prey as big as a young roe deer. It is a large bird, growing up to 70 cm long, is powerfully built, and has long ear tufts.

▼ TAKEAWAY MEAL
A barn owl holds on to a mouse it has just caught. Owls usually carry prey in their hooked bills, unlike other birds of prey, which carry it in their claws. Barn owls are found throughout most of the world and in various habitats — moorland, desert, forest and farmland.

barn owl
(*Tyto alba*)

▶ OFTEN HEARD, RARELY SEEN
A mouse is carried off by a tawny owl. The long, hooting, 'twit-twoo' call of this owl can be heard in woods, parks and gardens across Europe.

▲ PEEKABOO
A burrowing owl peers out of its nest hole. These small, long-legged birds live in the prairies and grasslands of the New World, from Canada to the tip of South America. They often take over the abandoned holes of other burrowers, such as prairie dogs.

Africa's Striped

1. From July to September, hundreds of thousands of animals follow the rains from the Serengeti in Tanzania towards the Masai Mara in Kenya. They move in long columns, following the same, well-worn paths every year.

Vast herds of zebras, gazelles and wildebeest roam the open plains of south and east Africa. They are constantly on the move, searching for better areas of grazing. The herds migrate from the acacia thorn forests in the north-west to the grasslands in the south-east, and back again. Their circular trip takes a year.

Zebras can sense a rainstorm from up to 100km away. They gather into large herds to watch for rain clouds and listen for thunder. The rain ensures the growth of plenty of new grass. Zebras are the first to arrive in these areas. They feed on the toughest parts of the vigorous new vegetation, paving the way for the more delicate grazers that follow.

2. One of the major obstacles on the great migration is the Mara River. No animal wants to take the plunge and cross first, as the river is filled with crocodiles. Enormous numbers of zebras and their travelling companions, wildebeest and gazelles, build up on the riverbank.

Migrators

3 When one animal starts to cross, the rest follow quickly. If the river is swollen by the rains, the animals must swim. Some are swept away in the torrent. Smaller members of the herd are pulled down and drowned by crocodiles. If the river is low, the zebras can wade across. They are quite capable of kicking an attacking crocodile with their hind feet and escaping.

4 Lionesses from a resident pride watch and wait among zebra and topi that have crossed the river. They will pounce on any floundering animal. The migrating animals offer a seasonal glut of food as they pass through the lions' territory.

5 The zebras have panicked at the scent of lions nearby and they abandon their river crossing. They will head back on to the plains, regroup and return to the river to try again. Somehow the zebras must cross to get to the new grass on the other side.

6 A lioness chases a scattered herd of zebra and antelope. The pride has fanned out and encircled the herd, chasing them towards an ambush. The migrating animals are followed by hyenas and nomadic lions on the lookout for stragglers and unprotected youngsters.

Trunk Tales

Imagine what it would be like if your nose and top lip were joined together and stretched into a long, bendy tube hanging down from your face. This is what an elephant's trunk must feel like. It can do everything that your nose, lips, hand and arm can do – and more besides. An elephant uses its trunk to breathe, eat, drink, pick things up, throw things, feel, smell, fight and play, squirt water, mud and dust, greet and touch other elephants and make sounds. Not surprisingly, a baby elephant takes a long time to learn all these ways to use its trunk.

▲ DRINKING STRAW
An elephant cannot lower its head down to the ground to drink so it sucks up water with its trunk. Baby elephants drink with their mouths until they learn to use their trunks to squirt water into their mouths.

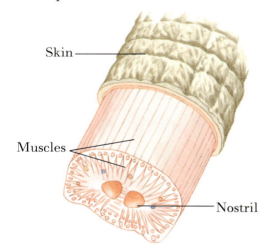

▲ A CLOSER LOOK
The two holes in the centre of the trunk are nostrils, through which the elephant breathes. Thousands of muscles pull against each other in different directions to move the trunk.

▲ WEIGHT LIFTER
An African elephant coils its trunk around a branch to lift it off the ground. Elephants can lift whole tree trunks in this way. The powerful trunk has more than 100,000 muscles, which enable an elephant to lift large, heavy objects easily.

TRUNK TALES

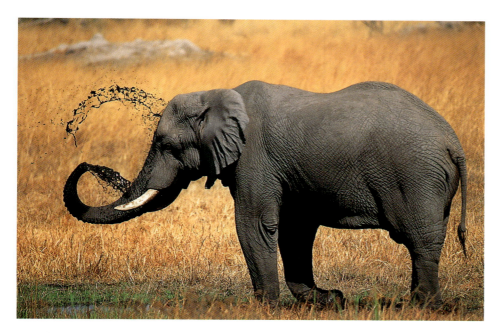

▲ TAKING A SHOWER
An elephant does not need to stand under a shower to be sprayed with water, mud or dust. Its trunk is like a built-in shower, able to cover almost its whole body as it reaches backwards over the head. Showering cools the elephant down and gets rid of insects.

▲ BENDY APPENDAGE
Elephants sometimes double up their trunks and rest them on their tusks. They can do this because the trunk has no bones inside it, just muscles, which makes it very flexible.

▶ TALL ORDER
African elephants use their long, stretchy trunks to pull leaves off the branches of tall acacia trees. The highest leaves are the most juicy. The trunk is slightly telescopic, which means that, if necessary, it can be stretched out even longer than usual. The trunk can also be pushed into small holes or gaps between rocks to find hidden pools of water.

Asian elephant

African elephant

▲ IDENTIFYING TIPS
The trunk of an African elephant has two fingers at the tip, while the Asian elephant has only one. These fingers can pick up an object as small as a leaf or a coin.

35

Jumbo

SPLASHING ABOUT
Elephants spray each other with water, wrestle with their trunks and flop sideways with great splashes. Sometimes they turn upside down and poke the soles of their feet out of the water. All this play strengthens the bonds between individuals and keeps groups together.

LIQUID REFRESHMENT
These two elephants are refreshing themselves at a waterhole. Elephants drink by sucking in water through their trunk. They seal off the end with the finger or fingers at the end of the trunk. Then they lift the trunk to the mouth and squirt in the water.

Elephants love water. They drink lots of it and enjoy going into lakes and rivers to play and splash around. Elephants are good swimmers and can easily cross rivers or swim out to sea to reach islands with fresh food. They drink at least once a day, or more often when water is available. When water is hard to find in the wild, elephants can be very sneaky, drinking from taps, pipes or water tanks. This usually causes damaged or broken pipes. Elephants can go without water for up to two weeks.

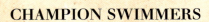

CHAMPION SWIMMERS
Elephants are good at swimming even though they are so big. When an elephant swims underwater, it pokes its trunk above the water and uses it like a snorkel to breathe through.

Water Babies

KEEPING CLEAN
Frequent bathing washes the build-up of mud and dust out of the cracks in an elephant's thick skin. Disease-carrying insects and parasites that feed off the elephant's skin are also washed off in the water.

HOLDING ON TIGHT
In the water, baby elephants often hold on to the tail of the elephant in front for safety. They can easily be swept away by fast-flowing rivers. Baby elephants are also vulnerable to attack from crocodiles.

THIRST QUENCHER
An elephant needs to drink 70–90 litres of water a day. A full trunk of water holds about 5–10 litres. Incredibly, a very thirsty adult elephant can drink about 100 litres of water in 5 minutes.

 BEARS

Great Navigators

Bears have an uncanny knack of finding their way home even in unfamiliar territory. How they do this is only just beginning to be understood. For long distances, they rely on an ability to detect the Earth's magnetic field. This provides them with a magnetic map of their world and a compass to find their way around. When closer to home, they recognize familiar landmarks. In fact, bears have extraordinary memories, especially where food is involved. For example, a mother and her cubs are known to have trekked 32km to a favourite oak tree to feast on acorns. Five years later, the same cubs (now adults) were reported to have been seen at the same tree.

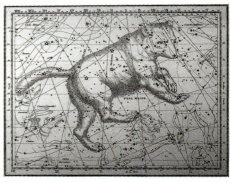

Stars in the Sky
The Great Bear constellation in the northern hemisphere is known to astronomers as Ursa Major. In Greek mythology, it was said to have been made in the shape of a she-bear and placed in the heavens by Zeus. The Great Bear is also worshipped in Hindu mythology as the power that keeps the heavens turning. The Inuit believe these stars represent a bear being continually chased by dogs.

▲ **ARCTIC NOMADS**
Polar bears are capable of swimming long distances between ice floes, at speeds of up to 10km/h. They may travel thousands of kilometres across the frozen Arctic Ocean and the surrounding lands in search of prey.

▲ **BAD BEAR**
A sedated polar bear is transported a safe distance out of town. Nuisance bears are often moved this way but they unerringly find their way back.

GREAT NAVIGATORS

◀ TO AND FROM THE FOREST

The polar bears of Hudson Bay, Canada, migrate to the forests in summer and return to hunt on the sea ice in winter. On their return journey, they sometimes stop off at the town of Churchill. They gather at the rubbish tip there to feed on leftovers, while they wait for ice to reform.

KEY

 Bears return to ice in winter

 Bears come ashore in June and July

 Bears walk north in autumn

▲ REGULAR ROUTES

Polar bears move quickly even on fast, shifting ice floes. A bear moving north, for example, against the southward-drifting ice in the Greenland Sea, can travel up to 80km in a day.

▲ RELYING ON MEMORY

Male brown bears live in large home ranges covering several hundred square kilometres. They must remember the locations of food and the different times of year it is available.

The Big Sleep

Black bears, brown bears and pregnant female polar bears sleep during the winter months. They do this because food is scarce, not because of the cold. Scientists have argued for years about whether bears truly hibernate or merely doze during the winter months and this argument still goes on today. During this sleep, or hibernation, a brown bear's heart rate drops to about 10 beats per minute. American black bears reduce their blood temperature by at least one degree. They do not eat or drink for up to four months. Bears survive only on the fat that they have stored during the summer months. A bear might lose up to half its body-weight before it awakes at the end of the winter.

▲ **FAT BEAR**
Before the winter sleep a bear can become quite tubby. Fat reserves make up more than half of this black bear's body-weight. It needs this bulk to make sure that it has enough fat on its body to survive the winter fast. In the weeks leading up to the winter, a bear must consume large quantities of energy-rich foods, such as salmon.

Did you know? Some hibernating bears sleep for 5½ months non-stop.

◄ **HOME COMFORTS**
A brown bear pulls in grass and leaves to cushion its winter den. American black bears and brown bears sleep in small, specially dug dens. These are usually found on the sunny, south-facing slopes of mountains.

THE BIG SLEEP

▲ FOREST REFUGE
A hole dug by a brown bear serves as its winter den in this Swedish forest. Bears spend winter in much stranger places, such as under cabins occupied by people, beneath bridges or beside busy roads.

▲ READY FOR ACTION
If disturbed, a bear wakes easily from its winter sleep. Although it is dormant, a bear's body is ready to be active. It is able to defend itself immediately against predators, such as a hungry wolf pack.

▲ SNOW HOUSE
Female polar bears leave the drifting ice floes in early winter and head inland to excavate a nursery den. They dig deep down into the snow and ice, tunnelling for about 5m to make the den. Here they will give birth to their cubs. In severe weather, male polar bears rest by lying down and allowing themselves to be covered over by an insulating layer of snow.

▲ WINTER NURSERY
In the early winter, one bear enters a den, but three might emerge in spring. Female polar bears, like most bears, give birth while hidden away in their dens. The tiny cubs (usually twins) are born in the middle of winter, in December or January.

Camouflaged Cats

A cat's fur coat protects its skin and keeps it warm. The coat's colours and patterns help to camouflage (hide) the cat as it hunts prey. Wild cats' coats have two layers — an undercoat of short soft fur and an outercoat of tougher, longer hairs, called guard hairs. Together these two layers insulate the cat from extreme cold or extreme heat. Some guard hairs are sensitive and help a cat to feel its way. Cats have loose skin, making it hard for an attacker to get a good grip and helping to prevent injury. The colours and patterns of a wild cat's coat depend on where it lives.

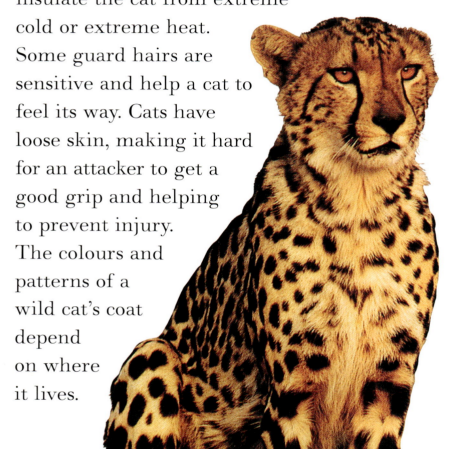

▲ TIGER IN THE GRASS
The stripes of a tiger's coat are the perfect camouflage for an animal that needs to prowl around in long grass. The colours and patterns help to make the cat almost invisible as it stalks its prey. These markings are also very effective in a leafy jungle where the dappled light makes stripes of light and shade.

Did you know? Domestic cats have a wider range of colours and markings than wild cats.

◀ KING OF THE HILL
King cheetahs were once thought to be different from other cheetahs. They have longer fur, darker colours and spots on their backs that join up to form stripes. Even so, they are the same species. All cheetahs have distinctive tear stripes running from the corners of their eyes down beside their muzzles.

CAMOUFLAGED CATS

▲ NON-IDENTICAL TWINS
Many big cats of the same species come in variations of colour, depending on where they live. These two leopard cubs are twins, but one has a much darker, blackish coat. Black leopards are called panthers. (Black jaguars and even pumas are sometimes called panthers.) Some leopards live deep in the shadows of the forest, where darker colouring allows them to hide more easily. Panthers are most common in Asia.

▼ SPOT THE DIFFERENCE
Spots, stripes or blotches break up the outline of a cat's body. This helps it to blend in with the shadows made by the leaves of bushes and trees, or the lines of tall grass. In the dappled light of a forest or in the long grass of the savanna, cats are very well hidden indeed.

A leopard's spots are in fact small rosettes.

The tiger has distinctive black stripes.

A jaguar has rosettes with a central spot of colour.

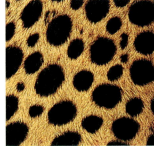
The cheetah has lots of spots and no rosettes.

◀ MOUNTAIN DWELLER
A snow leopard has a shaggy, off-white coat with darker spots. This colouring helps the snow leopard to stay well hidden in the rocky, mountainous terrain where it lives. It moves around early in the morning or late in the afternoon, blending with its habitat as it looks for prey.

A snow leopard's pale, thick coat has dark irregular spots and streaks. This helps the cat to hide between the rocks and snow.

The Dry Life

Deserts are very dry places. Although most are hot during the day, at night they are very cold. Few plants and animals can survive in such a harsh environment, but cats are very adaptable. Cheetahs, lions and leopards live in the Kalahari and Namib deserts of southern Africa. As long as there are animals to eat, the cats can survive. Even the jaguar, a cat that loves water, has been seen in desert areas in Mexico and the southern USA. But they are only visitors in this tough, dry land and soon go back to the wetter places they prefer. The best adapted cat to desert life is a small species known as the sand cat. It lives in the northern Sahara Desert, the Middle East and western Asia.

Did you know? Lions travel along dry riverbeds looking for waterholes in the desert.

▲ **DESERT STORM**
Two lions endure a sandstorm in the Kalahari Desert of southern Africa. The desert is a very hostile place to live. There is very little water, not much food and the wind blows up terrible sandstorms. Despite these hardships, big cats like these lions manage to survive.

This map shows where the world's hot deserts and nearby semi-desert areas are located.

▼ **A HARSH LIFE**
An old lion drinks from a waterhole in the Kalahari Desert. Even when a big cat lives in a dry place, it still needs to find enough water to drink. This is often a difficult task, requiring the animals to walk long distances. In the desert, prey is usually very spread out, so an old lion has a hard time trying to feed itself adequately.

THE DRY LIFE

▲ **CHEETAH WALK**
A group of cheetahs walk across the wide expanse of the Kalahari Desert. They lead lives of feast and famine. In the rainy season, some vegetation grows and herds of antelope can graze. The cheetahs have a banquet preying on the grazing herds. But they go very hungry as the land dries up and prey becomes scarce.

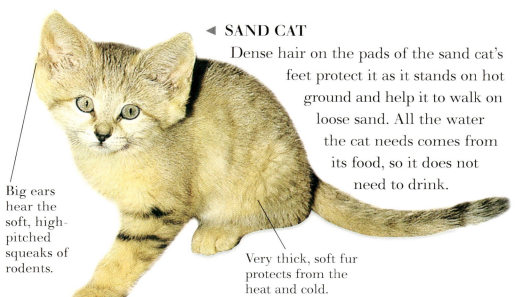

◀ **SAND CAT**
Dense hair on the pads of the sand cat's feet protect it as it stands on hot ground and help it to walk on loose sand. All the water the cat needs comes from its food, so it does not need to drink.

Big ears hear the soft, high-pitched squeaks of rodents.

Very thick, soft fur protects from the heat and cold.

▲ **ADAPTABLE LEOPARD**
A leopard rolls in the desert sand. There are very few trees in the desert, so leopards live among rocky outcrops. Here they can drag their prey to high places to eat in safety. The desert can be a dangerous place. With so little food around, competition can be fierce, especially with hungry lions. Big cats will eat small prey such as insects to keep from starving.

Egyptian Cat Worship
The Ancient Egyptians kept cats to protect their stores of grain from rats and mice. Cats became so celebrated that they were worshipped as gods. They were sacred to the cat-headed goddess of pleasure, Bast. Many cats were given funerals when they died. Their bodies were preserved, wrapped in bandages and richly painted.

WOLVES AND THEIR RELATIVES

black-backed jackal
(*Canis mesomelas*)

Fur Coats

Wolves and other members of the dog family have thick fur coats. This dense layer of hair helps to protect the animal's body from injury and keeps it warm in cold weather. Wolves and other dogs that live in cold places have extra-thick fur. Dingoes, jackals and wild dogs that live in warm countries close to the equator have sparser fur. The fur is made up of two layers. Short dense underfur helps to keep the animal warm. Long guard hairs on top have natural oils that repel snow and rain to keep the underfur dry. A wild dog's fur coat is usually black, white or tan, or a mixture of these. Markings and patterns on the fur act as camouflage to disguise these animals, so they can sneak up on their prey.

▲ **DISTINCTIVE OUTFIT**
The three species of jackal can be distinguished by their different markings. As its name suggests, the black-backed jackal has a dark patch on its back as well as brown flanks and a pale belly. The golden jackal is sandy brown all over. The side-striped jackal is so named because of the light and dark stripes that run along its sides.

◄ **WRAPPED UP WARM**
Two raccoon dogs shelter under a bush at the end of winter. Raccoon dogs are the only dogs in the world to hibernate. Their thick fur helps them survive through their long winter sleep. Originally from east Asia, raccoon dogs were brought to western Russia by fur farmers in the 1920s. Some escaped and they can now be found in eastern Europe.

FUR COATS

◀ MANES AND RUFFS
The maned wolf gets its name from the ruff of long hairs on its neck. This may be dark or reddish brown in colour. Wolves also have a ruff of longer hairs that they raise when threatened, to make themselves look larger.

▲ HANDSOME CAMOUFLAGE
African hunting dogs have beautiful markings, with tan and dark grey patches on their bodies, and paler, mottled fur on their heads and legs. The patterns work to break up the outline of their bodies as they hunt in the dappled light of the bush.

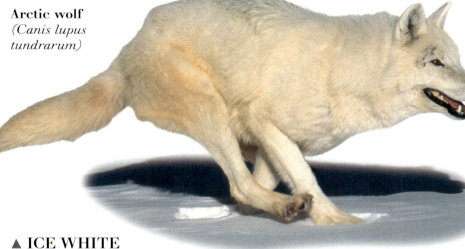

Arctic wolf
(Canis lupus tundrarum)

▲ ICE WHITE
The Arctic wolf has very thick fur to keep it warm in icy temperatures. Its winter coat is pure white so that it blends in with the snow. In spring, the thick fur drops out and the wolf grows a thinner coat for summer. This coat is usually darker to match the earth without its covering of snow.

VARYING COLOURS ▶
Grey wolves vary greatly in colour, from pale silver to buff, sandy, red-brown or almost black. Even very dark wolves usually have some pale fur, often a white patch on the chest.

grey wolf
(Canis lupus)

Snow Dogs

Wolves were once widespread throughout the northern hemisphere. As human settlements have expanded, so wolves have been confined to more remote areas such as the far north. The Arctic is a frozen wilderness where very few people live. Wolves and Arctic foxes are found here. On the barren, treeless plains known as the tundra, harsh, freezing winter weather lasts for nine months of the year. Both land and sea are buried beneath a thick layer of snow and ice. Few animals are active in winter, so prey is scarce. During the brief summer, the ice and snow melt, flowers bloom and birds, insects and animals flourish, so prey is abundant. Arctic wolves and foxes rear their cubs in this time of plenty. Another harsh, remote habitat, the windswept grass steppes of Asia, is home to the small steppe wolf.

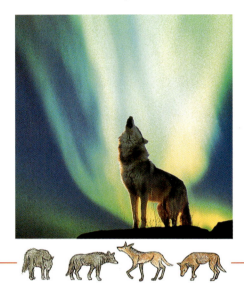

Arctic Legend
Native Americans named natural phenomena after the animals that lived around them. The Blackfoot people called the Milky Way the Wolf Trail. In Canada, the Cree believed the Northern Lights, shown below, shone when heavenly wolves visited the Earth. In fact these spectacular light shows in the Arctic are caused by particles from the Sun striking the Earth's atmosphere.

◀ **POLAR GIANT**
Arctic wolves are larger than most other wolves. They scrape under the snow to nibble plant buds and lichen if they are desperate for food.

Arctic wolf (*Canis lupus tundrarum*)

Did you know? The largest Arctic wolf territories cover 13,000 sq km—an area about the same size as Northern Ireland.

SNOW DOGS

▲ **COSY HOOD**
This Inuit girl is wearing a hood trimmed with wolf fur. The fur is warm and sheds the ice that forms on the hood's edge as the wearer breathes. The Inuit and other peoples of the far north traditionally dressed in the skins of Arctic animals. Animal skins make the warmest clothing and help to camouflage the wearer when hunting.

▲ **NORTHERN HUNTER**
A grey wolf feeds hungrily on a caribou carcass. In the icy north, wolves need very large territories to find enough prey. They will follow deer for hundreds of kilometres as the herds move south for the winter.

◀ **ARCTIC HELPERS**
One crack of a whip brings a team of huskies under control. Tough and hardy huskies, with their thick fur coats, are working dogs of the far north. They are used by the Inuit and other Arctic peoples to pull sleds and to help in hunting.

SNOWY BED ▶
A grey wolf shelters in a snowy hollow to escape a howling blizzard. With its thick fur, it can sleep out in the open in temperatures as low as -46°C. Snow drifting over its body forms a protective blanket.

Monkey Magic

Primates are the most versatile movers of the animal world. Many can walk and run, climb and swim. Small monkeys and the larger lemurs can leap between branches. This method is risky for larger animals, in case a branch breaks beneath their weight. Heavier primates play safe by walking along branches on all fours and avoid jumping if possible.

When branches are bendy, climbers move with caution. They may use their weight to swing from one handhold to the next, but they do not let go of one handhold until the other is in place. Tree-climbing monkeys have long fingers to curl around branches and help them to grip.

Monkeys that live on the ground use their hands as well as their feet to propel themselves along.

Did you know? A spider monkey's tail is so strong it can support the monkey's entire weight.

spider monkey
(*Ateles geoffroyanus*)

◄ **HANGING AROUND**
New World monkeys rarely move at ground level. Most swing from tree to tree, stop and whip their tail around a branch, let go with both hands and grab something to eat. Old World monkeys do not have a prehensile (grasping) tail. Many have very short tails or no tail at all.

◄ **PADDED MITTS**
The palm of a sifaka lemur is one of the features that makes it a star jumper. The wrinkles and fleshy pads are like a baseball glove, giving extra holding power. Sifakas can push off with their long hind legs to leap up to 5m high. Their arms are short, making it impossible to walk on all fours. Instead, sifakas hop on both feet.

MONKEY MAGIC

◀ **BABOONS ON THE MOVE**
A troop of baboons makes its way down a track in the African savanna. They are strong and tough because they have to walk long distances to find enough food to feed the troop. Baboons and other monkeys that walk on the ground, such as mandrills, geladas and macaques, put their weight on the fingertips and palms of their hands and feet. This is different from apes, such as gorillas and chimpanzees, who walk on their knuckles.

▲ **SLOW AND STEADY**
Lorises from Sri Lanka and southern India are known for their slow, deliberate movements. They have long, thin arms and legs with very flexible ankles and wrists. A loris can wriggle its way through, and get a grip on, dense twigs and small branches. Due to its strange appearance, some people describe the animal as a banana on stilts.

LIGHT AS AIR ▶
A pygmy marmoset can perch on the flimsiest of twigs. It has to be small, light and quick to catch the insects that it eats. Marmosets scurry along branches rather like squirrels, and for this reason are the only primates to have claws instead of nails. They are also able to sit up on their hind legs to free their hands for collecting food as well as for feeding.

51

APES

Hands and Feet

Can you imagine how difficult it would be to pick something up if your arms ended in paws, hooves or flippers? It would be impossible to grip any object and you could not turn it around, carry it, throw it, pull it apart or put it together. An ape's hands and feet are remarkable. They are very adaptable, and the opposable thumb or big toe enables them to grasp firmly or hold delicately. Ape hands and feet are strong and flexible, allowing apes to climb, swing and jump through the treetops. They also allow apes to reach food, investigate their surroundings, groom their family and friends and build nests. In most apes, the feet look very much like hands, but in humans, the feet look different. This is because human feet are adapted for walking rather than climbing.

▲ SMILE PLEASE
Grasping a delicate camera lens, a gorilla demonstrates how it can pick up fragile objects without breaking them. A gorilla has thicker, sturdier hands than a person, with fingers the size of bananas and a smaller thumb. Its hands have to be strong so that they can support the weight of the gorilla's body when it walks around on all fours.

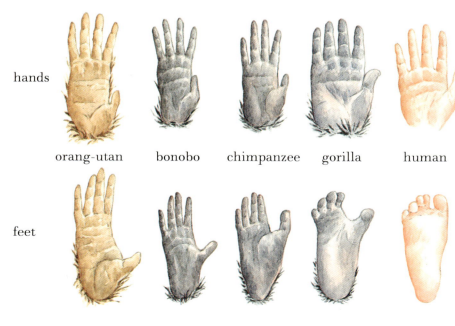

◀ LOOK-ALIKE HANDS
The hands of the great apes have several features in common, such as nails and long, sensitive fingers. The thumb on a great ape's hand goes off at an angle and can press against each finger. The big toe on an ape's foot can also do this, except in humans. Bonobos have a unique feature not shared by the other apes — webbing between the second and third toes.

HANDS AND FEET

Did you know? Humans have over 5 million hairs on their bodies.

orang-utan (*Pongo pygmaeus*)

▲ **OPPOSABLE THUMB**
Since a great ape's thumb can easily touch, or oppose, its fingers, it is called an opposable thumb. This special thumb gives an ape's hand a precise pincer grip, allowing it to pick up objects as small as berries.

▲ **GRAPPLING IRONS**
An orang-utan's arms and legs end in huge hands and feet that work like powerful clamps. Just one hand or foot can take the entire weight of the ape.

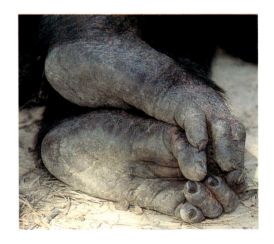

▲ **HAND-FOOT**
Unlike a human, a chimp can use its feet rather like hands, to hold and investigate things. The opposable big toe stretches out around one side of a branch while the toes reach around the other side, giving a very strong grip.

▲ **FLAT FEET**
Chimpanzees are flat-footed, with tough, hairless soles and long toes. When upright, their feet have to take all of the body weight.

Chimps

Humans were once thought to be the only animals clever enough to use tools. Now we know that a handful of other animals, such as Galapagos finches and sea otters, use them too. However, these animals are only beginners compared to chimpanzees. A chimp chooses its tools, changes them to make them better and uses them over and over again. Chimps plan ahead, collecting sticks or stones on their way to a source of food. Their nimble fingers and creative minds help them to invent and use tools. Adult chimps are good at concentrating, sometimes spending hours using their tools.

MAKING A TOOL
This chimpanzee is shaping a stick to help her dig for food. Chimpanzees have invented several clever ways to use sticks.

TASTY SNACKS
An intelligent chimp can shape and manipulate a grass stem to form a useful tool for fishing out termites from a mound. Scientists who have tried to copy the chimps have found that termite fishing is much, much harder than it looks.

FISHING FOR FOOD
This captive chimp is using a stick, in the same way as a chimp in the wild would use a grass stem, to fish in a termite mound. However, the termite mound in the zoo probably has yogurt or honey inside it, rather than termites.

That Use Tools

LEAF SPONGE
A wodge of leaves makes a useful sponge to soak up rainwater from tree holes. Chewing the leaf first breaks up its waterproof coating, so that it soaks up more water. Leaves may also be used as toilet paper, to wipe blood from wounds and to scrape up sticky food.

HANDY WEAPON
Wild chimps can only make tools from objects in their environment, which is why sticks are so important. Sticks make good weapons for attack and defence. They can also be used as levers, and thin sticks make a natural dental floss.

CRACKING PERFORMANCE
In West Africa, chimps use hammers and anvils to crack open the hard shells of nuts. Hammers are made from logs or stones, anvils from stones or tree roots. Hammer stones can weigh as much as 20kg. A skilled adult can crack a shell with just a few blows.

WHALES

Underwater Voices

Sounds travel easily in water. Whales use sounds to communicate with one another and to find their food. The baleen (filter-feeding) whales use low-pitched sounds, which have been picked up by underwater microphones as moans, grunts and snores. Dolphins and most other toothed whales communicate and hunt using higher-pitched clicks. They send out beams of sounds, which are reflected by objects, such as fish. The dolphin picks up the reflected sound, or echo, and can work out where the object is. This is called echo-location.

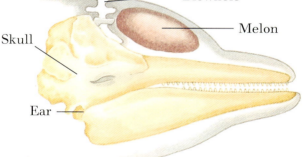

◀ ECHO SOUNDINGS
The Amazon river dolphin, or boto, hunts by echo-location. It sends out high-pitched clicking sounds, up to 80 clicks every second. The sound is transmitted in a broad beam from a bulge, called a melon, on top of its head.

▲ MAKING WAVES
A dolphin makes high-pitched sound waves by vibrating the air in the passages in its nose. The waves are focused into a beam by the melon. The sound is transmitted into the water.

▶ SEA CANARIES
A group of belugas, or white whales, swims in a bay in Canada. Belugas' voices can clearly be heard above the surface. This is why they are known as sea canaries. They also produce high-pitched sounds we cannot hear, which they use for echo-location.

UNDERWATER VOICES

◀ **SUPER SONGSTER**

This male humpback whale is heading for the breeding grounds where the females are gathering. The male starts singing long and complicated songs. This may be to attract a mate or to warn other males off its patch. The sound can carry for 30km or more.

▼ **WATER MUSIC**

This is a voice print of a humpback whale's song, picked up by an underwater microphone. It shows complex musical phrases and melodies. Humpback whales often continue singing for a day or more, repeating the same song.

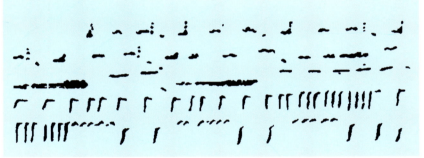

▼ **SOUND ECHOES**

A sperm whale can locate a giant squid more than a kilometre away by transmitting pulses of sound waves into the water and listening. The echo is picked up by the teeth in its lower jaw and the vibrations are sent along the jaw to the ear.

Did you know? A dolphin picks up sounds through its lower jaw.

◀ **ALIEN GREETINGS**

The songs of the humpback whale not only travel through Earth's oceans, but they are also travelling far out into Space. They are among the recorded typical sounds of our world that are being carried by the two Voyager space probes. These probes are now millions of kilometres away from Earth and are on their way far beyond our solar system.

SHARKS

frilled shark
(Chlamydoselachus anguineus)

Deep-sea Sharks

Many sharks are rarely seen because they live in the darkness of the deep. Catsharks and dogfish live in these gloomy waters, glowing in the dark with a luminous green-blue or white light. Some of these species travel and hunt in packs, following their prey to the surface at night and returning into the depths by day. Most of the world's smallest sharks live in the deep sea. Pygmy and dwarf sharks no bigger than a cigar travel for several kilometres through the ocean each day. On the deep-sea floor are enormous sharks such as the sixgill, sevengill and sleeper sharks. These eat the remains of dead animals that sink down from the sea's surface. Many deep-sea sharks look primitive, but strangest of all are the frilled and horned goblin sharks. These look like the fossilized sharks that swam the seas 150 million years ago.

▲ **LIVING FOSSIL**
The frilled shark is the only shark shaped like an eel. It has six feathery gill slits, 300 tiny, three-pointed teeth and a large pair of eyes. Like all sharks, it has a skeleton of flexible cartilage. These features show that the frilled shark resembles fossilized species that lived in the oceans millions of years ago.

▲ **DEEP-SEA TRAVELLER**
The shortnose spurdog can be recognized by a spine at the front of each dorsal fin. It lives in packs made up of thousands of sharks. It swims at depths of 800m in the northern waters of the Pacific and Atlantic oceans. At certain times of the year, the packs make a daily migration, from north to south and from coastal to deeper waters.

shortnose spurdog
(Squalus megalops)

▼ **DEEPEST OF THE DEEP**
The Portuguese dogfish holds the shark record for living in the deepest waters. One was caught 2,718m below the sea's surface. At this depth, the water temperature is no higher than a chilly 5–6°C.

Portuguese dogfish
(Centroscymnus coelolepis)

DEEP-SEA SHARKS

◀ SIX GILL SLITS
Most modern sharks have five gill slits, but primitive sharks, such as this bluntnose sixgill shark, have more. These species are found at huge depths around the world. They have evolved (developed) slowly, and still have the features of sharks that lived millions of years ago.

▼ SEVEN GILL SLITS
Broadnose sevengill sharks have seven gill slits. They have primitive, sharp teeth that look like tiny combs. They use these to slice up ratfish, small sharks and mackerel. Because some of their prey live near the surface, sevengill sharks travel up to the sea's surface to hunt at night.

broadnose sevengill shark
(*Notorynchus cepedianus*)

Did you know? Many deep-sea sharks have light organs on their bodies.

velvet belly
(*Etmopterus spinax*)

◀ SLIMY COAT
The velvet belly is 66cm long. It lives in the Atlantic and Mediterranean at depths of 70–2,000m. The velvet belly is covered with luminous slime, and the underside of its body has special organs that give out light. It eats deep-sea fish and shrimps.

Attack of

1 Huge groups of albatrosses nest on the ground close to the shore of Hawaiian islands, including the island of Laysan. The birds in each group breed, nest, and hatch their babies at the same time. When it is time, the young birds all take their first flight within days of each other.

Sharks can be found wherever there is food in or near the sea. Tiger sharks are rarely seen around some of the Hawaiian islands in the Pacific Ocean, but when the islands' young seabirds start to fly the sharks arrive suddenly. Any birds that fall into the sea are quickly eaten. The waters are too shallow for the tiger sharks to attack from behind and below as most sharks do. Instead, the sharks leap clear of the surface then drag the birds underwater to drown and eat them. Sharks arrive for their island feast at the same time each year. How they remember to do so is yet to be explained.

2 When ready to fly, a baby albatross practises by flapping its wings in the face of the islands' fierce winds. Eventually, the baby must make its first real flight over the ocean. When it does so, the tiger sharks are waiting in the water below.

3 Tiger sharks patrol the clear, shallow waters close to the albatross nests. Their dark shapes can be seen clearly against the sandy sea floor. Every now and again, a tiger shark's triangular dorsal fin and the tip of its tail can be seen breaking the water's surface.

the Tiger Sharks

4 Any baby bird that dips into the sea is prey for the waiting tiger shark. At first, the shark tries its usual attack, from below and behind. However, in the shallow waters the shark cannot make a full attack. Rather than hitting its prey at force, the shark just pushes the bird away on the wave made by its snout.

5 After failing to catch a meal, the shark soon realizes its mistake and tries another approach. Its next style of attack is to shoot across the surface of the water, slamming into its target with its mouth wide open. This technique seems to be more successful, and the shark usually catches the bird.

6 The shark then attempts to drag the bird below the surface, to drown it. If a bird is pushed ahead on the shark's bow wave, it will bravely peck at its attacker's broad snout and sometimes may even escape. Some birds also manage to wriggle free as the shark grapples with them underwater.

7 Many albatross babies do not manage to escape a shark attack. They are grabbed by the sharks and drowned. Inside the tiger shark's jaws are rows of sharp teeth that can slice into a bird's body like a saw. Sometimes the tiger shark tears off the bird's wings and leaves them aside to eat the body whole.

Glossary

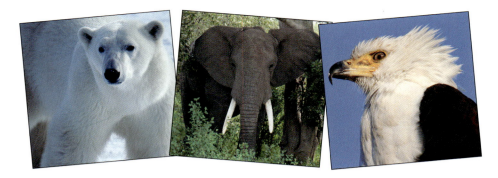

adapt
To change in some way in order to survive in altered conditions. This usually takes place over many generations in a process called evolution.

abdomen
The rear part of an animal's body where the reproductive organs and part of the digestive system are.

antennae
A pair of feelers on an insect's head, used mainly for smelling, but also for feeling things.

breed
An animal that belongs to one species, but has definite characteristics, such as colouring, body shape and coat markings.

camouflage
The colours or patterns on an animal's body that allow it to blend in with its surroundings.

carcass
The dead body of an animal.

carnivore
An animal that feeds on the flesh of other animals.

cold-blooded
An animal whose body temperature varies with that of its surroundings.

constrictor
A snake that kills prey by coiling its body around its prey to suffocate it.

crocodilian
A member of the group of animals that includes crocodiles, alligators, gharials and caimans.

digestion
The process by which food is broken down so it can be absorbed into the body.

echo-location
The method that toothed whales use to find their prey. They send out pulses of high-pitched sounds and listen for the echoes produced when the pulses are reflected by objects in their path.

environment
The conditions of an area an animal lives in.

equids
Horses and horse-like animals, such as asses and zebras.

evolution
The natural change of living organisms over very long periods of time, so that they become better suited to the conditions they live in.

filter-feeder
An animal that feeds by drawing a current of water over some kind of filter to strain out small particles of food.

fossil
The remains of a once-living plant or animal that have turned to stone over thousands or millions of years.

grazer
An animal that feeds on grass, e.g. a horse or antelope.

grooming
The way an animal cares for its coat and skin. It can be carried out by the animal itself or by one animal for another.

habitat
The kind of place where a group of animals live.

herd
A group of particular animals that remain together, such as elephants or wildebeest.

hemisphere
One half of the Earth, divided by the equator. The northern hemisphere lies above the equator, the southern hemisphere below it.

hibernation
A time when body processes slow down and an animal is inactive or sleeping during the cold winter months.

insect
An invertebrate (animal with no backbone) animal which has three body parts, six legs and usually two pairs of wings. Beetles, bugs and butterflies are all insects.

instinct
An inherited response to a particular stimulus that is common to all those in the same species. This is a response that is not taught to them but is a biological need, i.e animals use their instincts in hunting and reproduction.

larva (*plural* larvae)
The young of insects which undergo complete metamorphosis, such as beetles, butterflies and true flies. Larvae can be grubs, maggots or caterpillars.

keratin
A horny substance which makes up a snake's scales.

Latin name
The scientific name for a species. An animal often has many different common names. For example, the bird called an osprey in Europe is often referred to as a fish hawk in North America. The Latin name prevents confusion as it is used all over the world.

mammal
A warm-blooded animal with a backbone. Most have hair or fur. Mammals feed their offspring on milk from the mother's body.

migration
A regular journey some animals make from one habitat to another, because of changes in the weather or their food supply, or in order to breed.

muscle
An animal tissue made up of cells that can contract (shorten) to produce movement.

nocturnal
Active during the night.

paralyse
To make an animal powerless and unable to move, although it is still alive.

parasites
Animals, such as fleas and ticks, that live on other animals and harm them by feeding on them, although they do not usually kill them.

plain
An area of flat land without any hills.

predator
An animal that hunts and kills other animals for food.

prey
An animal that is hunted by other animals for food.

pride
A number of lions that keep together as a group.

raptor
Any bird of prey. From the Latin *rapere* meaning to seize, grasp or take by force.

species
Animals that belong to the same species are all so similar to each other that they can breed together successfully. Every different species has its own Latin name.

spinneret
An opening at the end of a spider's abdomen through which silk is pulled out.

stimulus
Something such as heat or light that causes a specific response in an organ in the body.

subspecies
A wide-ranging species may adapt to local conditions, and look different in some parts of the world. These different forms are called subspecies, but the animals are still able to breed together if they meet.

talon
A hooked claw, e.g. on a bird of prey.

territory
An area that an animal uses for feeding or breeding. Animals defend their territories against others of the same species.

venom
Poisonous fluid produced in the glands of some snakes and by nearly all spiders that is used to kill their prey.

warning colours
Bright colours, such as yellow and black stripes, indicate that an animal is poisonous. They warn predators to keep away.

warm-blooded
An animal that is able to maintain its body at roughly the same temperature all the time.

Index

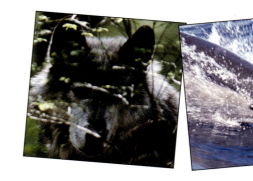

A
African hunting dogs 47
alligators 25, 26, 27
antennae 11
ants 10, 11
apes 5, 52–55

B
babies 25, 34, 37
baboons 51
basking 26, 27
bathing 35, 37
bears 4, 38–41
bees 10, 11
birds of prey 28–31
body temperature 10, 26, 27, 40
bonobos 52
brains 5
breathing 21, 34, 36
burrowing 10, 23, 31
butterflies 12–13

C
caimans 26
camouflage 42, 43, 46, 47
caterpillars 5, 12–13
cats 4, 42–45
cheetahs 4, 42, 44, 45
chimpanzees 5, 52, 53, 54–55
claws 10, 11, 30, 51
climbing 10, 11, 50, 51, 52, 53
communication 56–57
crocodiles 4, 5, 24, 25, 26, 27, 32, 33, 37

D
Darwin, Charles 6
defence 6–7
dens 27, 40, 41
deserts 44–45
digestion 20, 27
disguise 9, 15
displays 12, 47
dogs, wild 46–49
dolphins 56
drinking 34, 36, 37, 44, 55

E
ears 4, 30, 45
echo-location 56, 57
elephants 4, 34–37
evolution 4, 5, 6
eyes 4, 30, 58

F
feathers 4, 30
feeding 9, 15, 20, 21, 24, 25, 35, 54, 55
feet 10, 45, 52–53
fingers 50, 52, 53
fireflies 5, 8–9
flying 14, 28–9, 30
food
  chimpanzees 54, 55
  insects 9, 14, 15
  owls 30, 31
  sharks 58, 60–61
  snakes 20, 21
  spiders 16, 17
food, detecting 30, 38, 56, 57, 60
fur 42, 46, 47

G
gaping 26, 27
gazelles 32
gharials 25
glow-worms 8, 9
gorillas 52
gripping 10, 11, 22, 23, 30, 50, 52–53
grooming 10, 11, 52

H
hands 50, 52–53
hawk moths 14–15
hearing 30
hibernation 5, 27, 40–41,

I
insects 4, 6–15
instinct 5, 6

J
jackals 46
jaws 18, 20, 24–25

L
learning 5, 54
legs 10–11, 50, 51
lemurs 50
leopards 43, 44, 45
light, producing 8, 9, 58, 59
lions 33, 44
lorises 51

M
marmosets 51
mating 8, 19, 57
memories 38, 39
migration
  birds 5, 28–29
  mammals 32–33, 39
  sharks 58
monkeys 5, 50
moths 12–15
movement 10, 11, 39, 50, 51, 52, 53
  see also flying,
  see also swimming

N
navigation 38
night hunting 30

O
orangutans 52, 53
owls 4, 30–31

P
people
  and bears 38, 39, 41
  and dogs 49
  and spiders 18, 19
poison 6, 12–13, 17, 18–19, 20
polar bears 38, 39, 40, 41
predators 5, 6, 15, 31
primates 50–55
protection 6, 22, 42, 45

R
reproduction 9, 14, 41, 48

S
scales 22–23, 26
sharks 58–61
skin 22–23, 42, 49
smells 5, 6, 7, 12, 13
snakes 4, 5, 20–23
sounds 31, 56–57
spiders 5, 16–19
swimming 36, 38, 50, 60, 61

T
tails 7, 50
taste, repellent 6, 7, 12
teeth 24–25, 58, 59, 61
termites 10, 11, 54
tigers 42–43
tongues 14, 15
tools, using 5, 54–55
trunks 34–35

V
venom see poison

W
weapons 4, 6, 24, 55
whales 56–57
wildebeest 32
wings 8
wolves 46, 47, 48, 49

Z
zebras 32, 33

64